RISKY BUSINESS

Bomb Squad Officer

Expert with Explosives

By

KEITH ELLIOT GREENBERG

With Photography by Carol Halebian

A BLACKBIRCH PRESS BOOK

WOODBRIDGE, CONNECTICUT

Published by Blackbirch Press, Inc.
260 Amity Road
Woodbridge, CT 06525

©1996 Blackbirch Press, Inc.
First Edition

Printed in the United States of America

10 9 8 7 6 5 4 3 2 1

Photo Credits
Cover: © Spencer Grant/Photo Researchers, Inc.
Pages 4–5, 27: AP/Wide World Photos; pp. 7, 18–19, 18 (bottom inset), 20–21: Gamma-Liaison; pp. 10–11, 18 (top inset): Photo Researchers, Inc.

Library of Congress Cataloging-in-Publication Data

Greenberg, Keith Elliot.
    Bomb squad officer/by Keith Elliot Greenberg.—1st ed.
      p.   cm. — (Risky business)
    Includes bibliographical references and index.
Summary: Presents the life and career of Timothy Hajj, a bomb squad officer in Newark, New Jersey.
    ISBN 1-56711-155-6
    1. Bombing investigation—New Jersey—Newark—Juvenile literature. 2. Hajj, Timothy—Juvenile literature. 3. Police—New Jersey—Newark—Biography—Juvenile literature. [1. Hajj, Timothy. 2. Police—Special weapons and tactics units. 3. Bombing investigation] I. Title. II. Series: Risky business (Woodbridge, Conn.).
HV8079.B62G74   1995
363.2'5964—dc20
[B]   94-46244
                                                   CIP
                                                   AC

There didn't seem to be anything unusual about the man approaching the Newark, New Jersey bank—until he stepped up to the teller, placed a brown-paper package on the counter, and handed her a note.

The letter claimed that there was a bomb in the package. If the teller didn't immediately surrender cash, the man threatened to blow up the building.

A call was placed to the Newark Bomb Squad, and Sergeant Timothy Hajj soon arrived at the bank with two of his best explosives specialists.

3

Bomb squad officers must face the
danger of handling packages that
may contain powerful explosives.

"The bomb squad officers moved slowly toward the package—a paper bag with the top folded shut. They carefully peeled open the top flap. Because powerful bombs can be created with very small materials, officers can never be sure of what they will find.

"We don't know what they made," Timothy says. "We don't know what the explosives look like. We don't have a clue. And a piece of uranium the size of a golf ball could take out [Newark, New Jersey] and part of New York."

Fortunately, Timothy and his squad faced no such danger on this call. There was nothing inside the bag but a soda bottle.

"Your heart's been beating fast," he says. "Lights and sirens have been going off. It's mayhem. You can be exhausted by the time you're finished."

To many people, Timothy is a hero. Still, he never makes the mistake of being overconfident. For any bomb squad officer, one misstep can be deadly.

Timothy (left) looks over some explosives with Captain John Kossup.

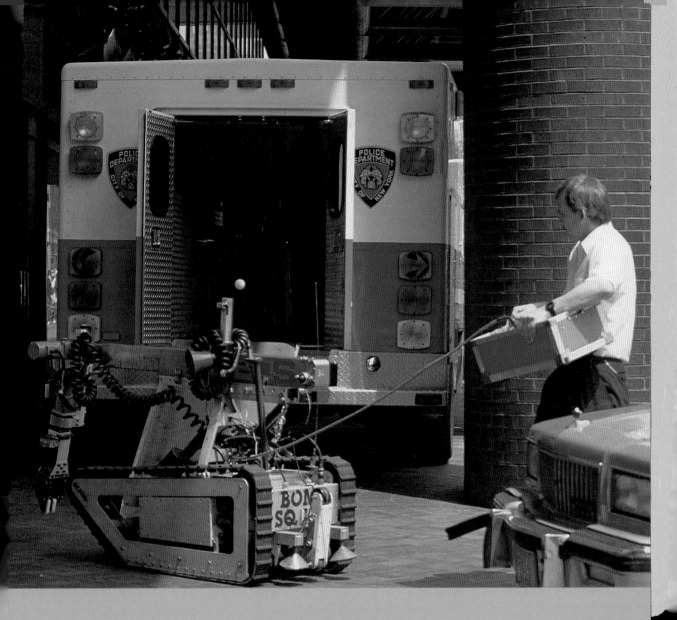

"It's a dangerous job," says Timothy's boss, Captain John Kossup. "Sometimes just moving an object, or a change in weather conditions, can set off a bomb. You can't take anything lightly."

A bomb squad officer unloads a special robot used to capture potential explosives.

In the large city of Newark being a bomb squad officer is particularly challenging. Bombing targets are everywhere. The shipping port is one of the largest in the world. The international airport serves not only New Jersey, but also nearby New York City. At the Martin Luther King Federal Courthouse, international terrorists and mobsters are often put on trial.

Potential bomb targets
are everywhere, includ-
ing airports, federal
buildings, and seaports.

A high-tech police robot
handles a live bomb by
remote control.

Timothy was 19 years old when he joined the Newark Police Department. Because of his street smarts and youthful look, he was quickly made an undercover narcotics officer.

At 28, Timothy became the youngest sergeant in the history of the Newark Police Department. As a supervisor in the Emergency Services division, he oversees rescues in the city's waterways, the medical response team, the mounted—or horseback—unit, and the bomb squad.

"Most of the bomb calls we get are pranks," he admits. "But we still have to go."

"We have to investigate everything," Timothy says.

Timothy displays some
of the dangerous items
his department has
found in the past.

Timothy is constantly amazed by the types of weapons he finds. Searches have turned up military weapons, such as shrapnel-firing hand grenades and grenades that discharge tear gas.

Some pipe bombs are made in homes, using matches, wiring, gauze, and a pipe. Other people create explosives by mixing chemicals. Some Newark citizens have been sent bombs in packages with devices designed to shoot out nails and glass.

Homemade bombs are common threats and can be quite powerful.

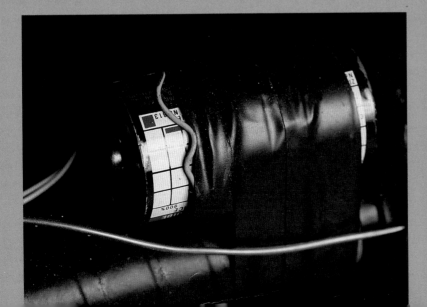

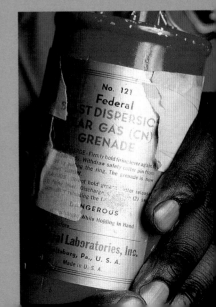

Timothy speaks with the mayor of Newark, Sharpe James, about security for an upcoming political function.

When politicians or other important people gather in Newark, the bomb squad is always especially careful. "If a ballroom is being set up, you let them put in all the flowers, all the gifts, all the plaques," Timothy explains. "Then, you close off the room. No one goes in. No one goes out. You bring in the bomb-sniffing dogs, and the bomb squad. Every member gets a section of the room. You inspect everything you see: the bottoms of tables, boxes, bundles, the bottom of the podium. Then, when you know things are alright, you let the people come in."

Specially trained dogs are often used by
bomb squads to sniff out explosives.

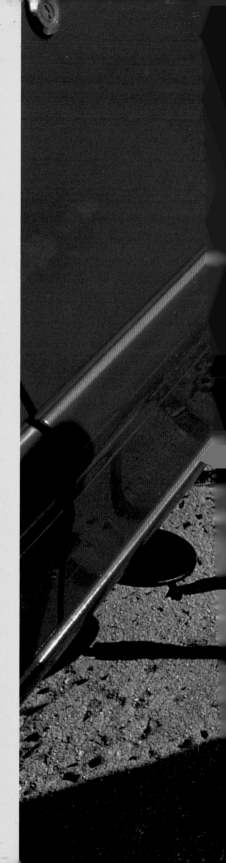

In 1994, the Newark Police Department purchased a 28-foot boat to patrol Newark Bay, the Passaic River, and the city's port. These areas can be prime locations for bombs. When drugs are found on vessels or cargo, bombs are sometimes also nearby.

Some drug dealers have used powerful electromagnets to attach drugs to the bottoms of their pleasure boats. If caught, the smugglers don't want to leave any evidence. So they booby-trap the drugs with bombs.

Police divers are called in to search the vessels for unusual bulges. Since any type of movement can trigger the explosives, the bomb squad must take the weapons apart very carefully.

16

A mirror on a long handle is one device bomb squad officers use to inspect the underside of motor vehicles.

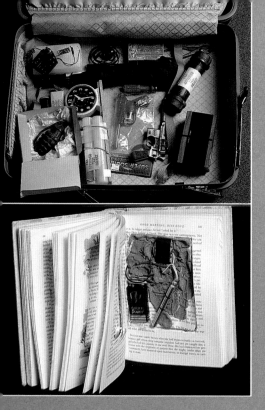

Insets: Certain types of bombs are so small and hard to find that they can be hidden almost anywhere. Below: The ruins of a Pan Am plane that was blown out of the sky over Lockerbie, Scotland, by a bomb no bigger than a tennis ball.

At the busy Newark Airport, finding a bomb can be incredibly difficult. Bombs look like many items going through the x-ray machine: tape recorders, clocks, video games. And certain kinds of bombs don't register on a metal detector. "You can shape a plastic explosive to look like anything," Timothy says. "It doesn't have to be big to be dangerous. A plastic explosive the size of a tennis ball could blow a plane out of the sky."

In February 1993 and then April 1995, two devastating explosions rocked the United States and struck sadness and fear into millions of Americans. In 1993, a massive car bomb destroyed the underground garage of the World Trade Center in New York City, injuring many people and threatening the lives of thousands. In 1995, more than 160 people were killed when a homemade bomb destroyed the Federal Building in Oklahoma City, Oklahoma.

 Bomb squad personnel survey the scene at the World Trade Center after the blast.

Rescue workers
search the rubble
of the Federal
Building in
Oklahoma City.

The bomb squad uses a special truck that is equipped with tools for bomb disposal.

The police department responds to calls by first sending a patrol car to investigate. If an officer finds anything unusual, no one is permitted to touch it.

If something appears dangerous, the officer contacts the bomb squad. If possible, a regular telephone is used. Radio waves from a cellular phone or walkie-talkie can activate a bomb.

The bomb squad comes to the scene in a special bomb truck. "I tell my men to drive carefully," Timothy says. "If we kill 20 people on the way because we crashed into a bus, the bomb is still there, and we didn't do our job."

Inside the bomb truck, there's an x-ray machine that is used to see through packages. The truck is also equipped with metal prongs used to pick up dangerous objects.

The bomb truck pulls a special bomb trailer—a heavy metal cylinder on wheels. If a bomb is about to explode, it might be thrown into the cylinder. The sandy substance inside muffles the blast. The top of the cylinder is always removed—so it doesn't blow through the air like a giant steel frisbee.

A bomb cylinder is used to explode bombs in an emergency.

A bomb squad officer sets up an x-ray device used to inspect potentially dangerous packages.

One officer puts on a special bomb suit made of heavy material that can weigh up to 85 pounds.

To be sure that they're looking at a bomb, the technicians will search for several signs: wires, a battery or other source of power, and a device that will detonate (set off) the weapon.

A member of the bomb squad may wear a special 85-pound bomb suit, as the weapon is taken apart. "It's supposed to protect you from the blast, but that doesn't mean you won't get hurt," Timothy says. "You'll still get knocked 50 or 60 feet away from where you started. You'll be all bruised up. You just won't be dead."

Below left: Batteries, wires, and other sources of power can be tip-offs to bombs. Below: Bomb suits are worn by officers who must get in close to potential explosives.

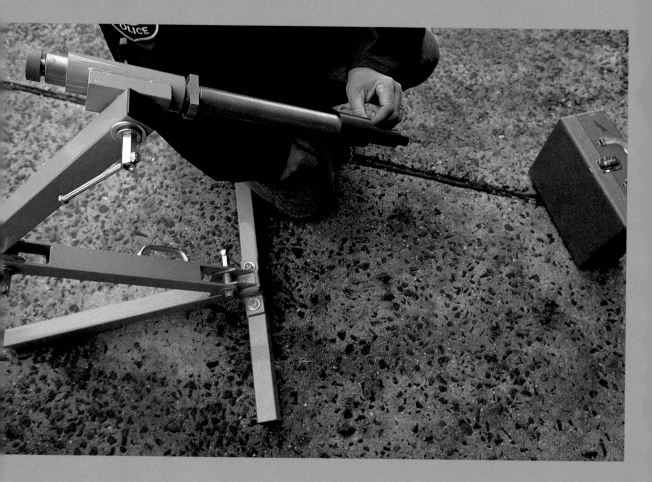

A disrupter gun disarms batteries by shooting them with lead.

Before they explode a bomb on purpose, officers will first take many steps to try to disable it. For example, the squad will use a disrupter. This is a special gun that destroys a battery by firing lead into it.

Another tool can hit a bomb with a forceful burst of water. "It's so powerful that the water can penetrate a box or a light metal case," Timothy says. "If you were struck by the water, it would kill you."

Once the squad is satisfied that a device has been disarmed, the object is x-rayed again to make sure no part of it is working. Then, just to be safe, it is transported in a special basket made of bullet-proof material to a firing range and blown up.

Laser scopes and simple bomb baskets are both valuable tools for the bomb squad.

Concentration may be the most important quality of a bomb squad member. "Pay attention," Timothy stresses. "You have two ears for listening, two eyes for watching, and just one mouth for talking. That should tell you that observation [and listening are] more important than talking."

Many people in Newark think it's nice to know that a man like Timothy Hajj and his officers are on the job. They feel safe in the knowledge that their lives and their community are being protected by brave and well-trained people who really care about helping others.

Bomb squad officers like Timothy Hajj put their lives in danger to protect others.

FURTHER READING

Dick, Jean. *Bomb Squads & Swat Teams*. New York: Crestwood, 1988.

Emert, Phyllis R. *Law Enforcement Dogs*. New York: Crestwood, 1985.

Greenberg, Keith. *Terrorism*. Brookfield, CT: The Millbrook Press, 1994.

Kerson, Adrian. *Terror in the Towers: Amazing Stories from the World Trade Center Disaster*. New York: Random Books, 1993.

McPherson, Jan. *The Dog School*. Austin, TX: Raintree/Steck-Vaughn, 1990.

Smith, Carter. *A Day in the Life of an FBI Agent-in-Training*. Mahwah, NJ: Troll, 1991.

INDEX